Selected Poems & the Lost Drabbles

Steven J. Scott

MAPLE
PUBLISHERS

Selected Poems & The Lost Drabbles

Author: Steven J. Scott

Copyright © Steven J. Scott (2024)

The right of Steven J. Scott to be identified as author of this work has been asserted by the author in accordance with section 77 and 78 of the Copyright, Designs and Patents Act 1988.

First Published in 2024

ISBN 978-1-83538-218-9 (Paperback)
       978-1-83538-219-6 (E-Book)

Cover Design and Book Layout by:
    White Magic Studios
    www.whitemagicstudios.co.uk

Published by:
    Maple Publishers
    Fairbourne Drive, Atterbury,
    Milton Keynes,
    MK10 9RG, UK
    www.maplepublishers.com

A CIP catalogue record for this title is available from the British Library.

All rights reserved. No part of this book may be reproduced or translated by any form or by any means, electronic or mechanical, including photocopying, recording or by any information storage and retrieval system without written permission from the author.

The views expressed in this work are solely those of the author and do not necessarily reflect the views of the publisher, and the publisher hereby disclaims any responsibility for them.

CONTENTS

Part 1 – Ten Thousand Rhymes Ago

1. The Bookshop 8
2. Cobblestones 10
3. Our Time 11
4. Stalker 12
5. Sealed Off 13
6. Caliban 14
7. Hurt Again 15
8. Seeking the Sage 17
9. Old Friends 18
10. Seven Deadly Longings 20
11. Lauds 22
12. Gypsy Tale 23
13. Change 25
14. Friendship 26
15. Van Gogh 27
16. The Pen & the Sword 29
17. The Fisherman 30
18. Winter Blues 31
19. Casualty 33
20. Ghost Writer 34

21. War Crime (The Somme, 1916) 35
22. Squirrel in the Park 37
23. Hallowe'en 38
24. Stars 40
25. Ten Thousand Rhymes Ago 41

Part 2 – Tapestries

26. Residue 44
27. Among My Papers 45
28. October 46
29. 'Ugly' 47
30. Mercutio 48
31. The Waiting 50
32. Flower Girl 52
33. Scrooge 53
34. Bill Sikes 54
35. In the Reptile House 55
36. Diesel 56
37. Dry-Dock 58
38. Raptors 59
39. Debris 60
40. Tapestries 61
41. Hamlet 62

42. Barbarians 63
43. The Ninth Legion 65
44. Grendel 66
45. Museum...67
46. Spider 68
47. Snow 69
48. The Haunting of Emily 70
49. Love Song in the Night (New York, 1942) 71
50. Odyssey..73

The Lost Drabbles
- Sammy Squirrel Takes a Risk
- Mr. Po's Old Comrade
- The Seventh Gate
- The Dream Tea of the Emperor Hu
- Spider & Fly
- The City of Tears
- The Duchess's Diamonds
- Sour
- Dreadful Penny
- The Ogre's House
- The Captain's Table
- Arena

- The Witch
- Loose Ends
- The Trail
- Demon Drive
- The Hunt
- The Archive
- Between Stations
- Panic at Dodge City!
- Smith & Jones
- Smith & Jones (Part 2)
- Smugglers
- Decorating
- Geometry
- Crooked
- Code of Honour
- Pebbles
- Tresses
- Step

SELECTED POEMS
Part 1
Ten Thousand Rhymes Ago

Steven J. Scott

The Bookshop

I'd go there almost every day
in my lunch break to browse the shelves

I'd pause at the books laid out on the tables
marvelling at the fantastic covers
and wondrous displays –
familiar authors stirring my memory to a childhood
full of outlandish characters with outlandish names
involved in perilous plots with menacing villains
and faithful friends
in fantasy worlds more real than our own
where the monsters always lost in the end …

And beside me some children would whoop
in surprise, as a picture book opened
and the dragon was slain
and looking on, an old lady smiled
(while mum was noisily hushing them quiet)

So I'd slowly pace back past the reference books
and behind the counter they'd shake their heads
"It's him again! I thought he was barred –
he spends more time here than he does at work!"
and my grin turned into a guilty laugh

But now there's only another boarded up shop
just a nothingness left on the streets –
estate agents and discount stores
selling empty containers and half-price sweets

And looking back through the years
with the eyes of a child
I feel suddenly old …
for the dreams have all gone
and the monsters have won

and all of our stories are told.

Cobblestones

Among a labyrinth of cobblestones
a man with a rose walks slowly by

Wind sweeps along the alley streets
swirling the dust beneath his feet
as he turns down the steps

To the underground, where the city
crawls to a deadpan beat that never rests –

Expressionless, he clutches the rose,
hanging onto a subway train
the weight of the day leans on him, needing only
to see her face …

And escaping from the world below, he traces a path
on the cobblestones of his hometown
and touches the gate
handing his love, this special rose

That lights her smiling, sparkling eyes
in the softly falling rain.

Our Time

My time is passing
so slowly
today
I gaze bemused
at the clock on the wall
and then suddenly
it's gone
all over –
and I wonder -
how much
time
we really
have
left
at
all?

Stalker

From behind these shades I'm watching you
following your every move

Seeing everything you see
knowing everything you do

All your family and friends
every number on your phone

I shadow you in your dreams at night
company when you're alone

And in the morning I'll be there
quietly waiting on your street

From behind these shades I'm watching you
you'll never get away from me.

Sealed Off

I'd rather not get too close to his mind –
the killer's

We all saw the crime scene
walls spattered like child's paint
in a game that had ended horribly wrong

We took the samples, prints, photographs
not trusting our senses

(torn and torn and torn into pieces –)

And emerged into bright sunshine
faces white in disbelief

Birds sang and the world seemed normal
but something inside us was gone for ever

Wordlessly, we set the barricades
and then just stood there

Separate from the growing crowd
sealed off.

Caliban

Before the tempest wracked these shores
this island was my paradise

Betrayed by cruel sorcery
I watched the old gods fade and die

And now I'm nothing but a slave –
a wretched monster – savage – beast!

Tormented at a tyrant's whim
and plagued by unseen miseries

A strange new world, so brave and free
how is it I am still alone?

A thing of darkness I've become
my heart as heavy as a stone

But sometimes through enchanted dreams
sweet voices whisper in my ears

And fill my soul with such wonders
that waking … I weep bitter tears.

Hurt Again

He sits alone in his apartment
used to his own company
happy with a life of freedom
he needs no one to share his dreams

Sometimes the shadows fall on him
but all in all he does not complain

Oh yes, he leads a lonely life
not wanting to be hurt again ...

She sits alone in her apartment
used to her own company
happy with a life of freedom
she needs no one to share her dreams

Sometimes the shadows fall on her
but all in all she does not complain

Oh yes, she leads a lonely life
not wanting to be hurt again ...

They pass each other on the street
a nervous glance, then turn away

Oh yes, they lead a lonely life
not wanting to be hurt again.

Seeking the Sage

High in the mountains
I seek the reclusive sage

Only to find his essence is lost
In the surrounding beauty of this wilderness.

Old Friends

An October day, overcast, with drizzly rain
falling incessantly on everything
All over London life has stirred, and two old friends
are about to meet, for the first time in so many years …

Johnson drags a dampened matchbox
from the false pocket of his ancient coat
Crossing over traffic lights, he leans on the wall
to light his smoke

Jones stumbles out of café, nondescript
eggs and bacon all the same, yawning in the morning rain
He sits on bench and ponders life, in his torn and ragged suit
that's seen much better days

An image forms in Johnson's mind –
marching rows of faceless men, rifles pointing at the sky
and then all turning straight to him
Now he sees the battered trenches, in battle's ruddy afterglow
trying to stay alive another day and night –
and a friend who once had saved his life …

Jones finishes his warm weak beer, and wanders through Soho's

grimy streets. By the underground in Piccadilly, a newspaperman

is peddling sheets – read all about the latest crisis

but nobody pays any heed

Johnson stares at the ground, studying the pavement cracks

he sees a shadow pass him by – and suddenly stops in his tracks

"Jones! Is that you? It can't be ... Jones?"
"Johnson? No ...!"

And they reach out, clasping hands and arms
neither one able to speak

Jones the first to recover –
"Pint?"

Johnson scratching in his pockets
"Cup of tea," he sighs, with threadbare smile ...

Steven J. Scott

Seven Deadly Longings

The drunkard is longing, for just one more drink
the Proud looks on, with a righteous grin

The artist is longing, for a reason to live
the Covetous aches, for his special gift

The miser longs, for more money to hoard
the Lustful sees nothing, but wants it all

The businessman longs, to close on the deal
the Envious curses his neighbour's fields

The lawyer longs, for another soft case
the Gluttonous quickly, piles up his plate

The singer longs, for that one special note
the Angry grabs all but himself by the throat

The victim longs, to forget what he saw
the Slothful's too idle to care any more

And as I silently pass, my whole world spinning round
I'm longing to see, just one face in the crowd

I'm longing to hold her, not letting her go
still committing the sin, of needing her so.

Lauds

All is quiet, my blood so thin
against the coldness of this cell
the night has passed, wretchedly

nerves entwined with bitter dreams

In the distance I hear morning prayers
from the little church upon the hill
sunlight climbs above these stones

but memories enslave the soul

Soon this darkness will be over
I am guilty and must pay the price
footsteps falter at my door

they tie my hands and lead me out

A crowd has gathered silently
the lonely hangman looks away
can there ever be forgiveness?

from the hill I hear them pray …

Gypsy Tale

Last night when I was dreaming
a story came to me, from a time
belonging somewhere in my childhood

Piecing itself together, through scattered
anecdotes and imagery – tales so tall
told by gnarled old men

smoking quietly around campfires
when I was just a boy – and the world
so young and free

And the misty breath of the tired horses
hung like clouds in the twilight air
their heads lowered as if they too

were listening to the words, loosely tethered
by the sleeping wagons, their unhooked
noses trailing in the dirt ...

And as the story wove itself around us

and the world grew large in our young minds
we drifted away to the distant heavens

of a dazzling sky, with its
eternal eyes that brought us light
through the passion of the swirling stars.

Change

On a bustling street
the old man plays
with a sad half-smile
& life-filled eyes
the accordion swirls
its ragged tune

melancholy
        beautiful

& I stop to listen
for a while
to shelter from
the falling rain
his upturned cap
recalls the past –
where people drop
their forgotten
change.

Friendship

How can it be after all this
long time
that such a simple thing
can bring a tear
to the eye
when all else has failed
to move us?

Is it because
we're so blindly immune
to all of life's states
to all
that the fates
can crush out of us
with their endlessly see-sawing whirligig wheels?

Or is it just that despite all of this
we're here to laugh at the world,
so absurd in its twists
over a couple of beers
and a noggin of gin
both of us greyer and balding in years
here's to it lasting, my friend!

Van Gogh

They said I was a dreamer
and wasted all my days
Tracing the boats' reflections
in the waters of the Seine

They said I was an idler
with canvas under arm
From the teeming streets of Paris
to the orchard groves of Arles

I saw the world through imagery
in blazing colours all afire
I saw peasants toiling in the fields
in a land that was so dry

I saw poverty and suffering
and felt the anguish of the damned
Knew the loneliness of hunger
and the humbleness of man

I wore the weary boots of destiny
and in the landscapes of my mind
Saw the beauty and the solitude
the sleepy town and starry sky

I painted all that I beheld
but my pain was growing worse
And in an instant of despair
my art became my curse.

The Pen & the Sword

The sword might be sharper
but the pen is more blunt

The sword might be heavy
but the pen weighs a ton

The sword might be piercing
but the pen sees it all

The sword might be pointed
but the pen's on the ball!

The sword might be trusty
but the pen don't believe

The sword might be drawn
but the pen can deceive

The sword might be bloodied
but the pen has destroyed

The sword might be keener
but the pen is annoyed!

Steven J. Scott

The Fisherman

... sits waiting by the riverbank
where nothing seems to bite today

life's flotsam slowly drifting by
determined not to take the bait

but no, it doesn't bother him –
hat discarded with waterproofs

he only wants to pass the time
and drown his mind

in solitude.

Winter Blues

I'm weary to my soul tonight, my bones stretched out
as the dust settles on a fading skyline

somehow I feel

my life receding, like a fog slinking out of a barroom night
leaving only the distant mutter of those left behind
still drinking in the shadows

My hollow room crowds me out, with a longing for ... peace
I cannot find the words

through this dampening lamplight and coffee headache
the dragging of the chain-smoked hours
... and the quiet jangling of my nerves

Ancient blues from beat club in town, pours out its heart
into the rain

plaintive strains
on base and treble ... winter blues ... drifting through
the garbage-can alleys of our city heights
low meter running, dimming bloodshot lights

filling the night with a last farewell ...
bringing a tear to my
sunset eyes.

Casualty

He died of life at 4am
well after the pubs had turfed out
the trash
and I sat by his side
on a groggy street, in the midst of an evil
winter night
watching his life fade away ...
alone I heard his clattering breath
a few broken words before the end

there were two casualties in town that night
and no one mourned for them.

Ghost Writer

Sometimes I feel I'm writing in the dark
writing someone else's story

deep into the night

Writing in the gloom
like the mad woman in the attic room

Just waiting for the fit to pass
hoping and praying it will not last

and longing for the dawn ...

War Crime
(The Somme, 1916)

After that last horrific skirmish
we cleaned the mud from our ruined boots
& I leaned inside a molten trench
too tired now to even move
& the sergeant muttered breathlessly
that we should fight no more
we'd given every bloody thing we had
upon this hateful
battlefield

& he told us of a dream he'd had
through the remnants of a cigarette
of a world where there was no war
with friends all dead & leaders lost
& we talked into the patchy air
of how things were before
& told stories – some made up I'm sure
& passed the endless hungry night
in the bitter cold so strange & dark

In the dawn they came for us again
& the sky lit up in the burning rain
& I was so scared I wasn't scared no more

& the sergeant couldn't speak, just stare
but when the bugle sounded from afar
we knew this was our final charge
& went over – never knowing
why.

Squirrel in the Park

So quickly he scrambles
across fences and trees
nervously twitching
digging his hoard
one blink
and he's gone!
no time to rest –
his energy stored
in suburbia's sprawl

And just when you think
that you've lost him
for good
and you cannot connect
the gulf is too wide –
he's there at your feet
looking straight up at you
with the rain in his fur
and the world in his eyes.

Hallowe'en

Are the ghosts and demons out tonight
do you feel them crawling down your spine –
do you sense dark magic in the air
harrowing your tired mind?

October's chill cuts to the bone
pumpkins grin at summer's end
you're wandering late, cold and alone
as the spirits gather, for reunion

The veil between the worlds is thin
pagan festivals invite the dead
you listen closely as the old gods stir
and wrap your cloak tight to your chest

The circle's closing in on you
beckoning … to a darker realm
a sacrifice to a dying sun
calls all souls to the Underworld

You try to shake their mad pursuit
but inside you know it's just too late
you panic, cry out in the night –
but you've already gone astray

With dim relief you reach your door
black cats cross an eerie street
strange shapes uncoil from your welcome mat
and embrace you on All Hallows Eve ...

Stars

What do you think, my love?
they say I should cut my hair
and live like a monk
they say I shouldn't waste time
on things that can't last
that I should follow the rules –

and forget that I saw you
among the stars.

Selected Poems & The Lost Drabbles

Ten Thousand Rhymes Ago

At half past nine
I entice a cold one
from the fridge
and try to conjure up
a line or so

(in between I think of you
ten thousand rhymes ago)

At half past ten
I'm struggling through another verse
I cannot quite conclude
and as I meditate upon the muse
my doubts begin to grow

(for I'm thinking only of your face
ten thousand rhymes ago)

Half past eleven
and I'm rescuing
a phoenix from a dying flame
but my concentration's gone astray
my mind's on overflow

(for I'm tasting still our bitter pain
ten thousand rhymes ago)

At half past twelve
I cannot sleep
wishing I could take a stronger dose
and turn back time to another place
when I could feel your body glow

(as we held each other – oh so close!
ten thousand rhymes ago).

SELECTED POEMS
Part 2
Tapestries

Residue

And we just … talked
my old friend's shaking hand
still lingering
on the fingertips
of our unspoken understanding

January … and so cold outside
the ice still clung to a thawing heart
slowly beating, between the warmth
of our fading smiles

(drawn closely in the dimming light
of the all-night café bar)

And the night was tugging
at memories, and sorrow misting
our tired minds

A nameless emotion had filled my eyes
and left me there
inside the past's half remembered
aching tune
more strangely real, than life is now,
now all that's left
is residue …

Among My Papers

Among my papers I found a note
a few lines scribbled hurriedly

nothing special, only words
except they were from you to me

I'd forgotten the wounds of yesterday
how our dreams went up in smoke

I'd locked the past away from view –
until among my papers

I found your note.

October

It's so quiet here
only bleak isolation
surrounding these fields

The eye of Nature looks into itself
and clouds start to gather
in dark looming hills

I pace across an open meadow
where the threat of winter
is a breath away –

And reach the old farmhouse
with rain beating down
and a desolate wind stinging my face

The gate strains and groans
on its hinges
my hand unsteady as I fumble the key

Perhaps it is just a feeling I have
or maybe October is calling
to me …

'Ugly'

Her mouth is too tight & her figure too thin
She lives in a bedsit too small to live in
Her hair is too straggly & her eyes are too big
She rolls her own tabs & she drinks like a fish!

She works where she can, she needs no career
Her ambition is simple – it's now & it's here!
She's trying to study – she's making a start
She watches old movies but doesn't dig art

She's a little bit reckless, but causes no pain
A little bit scatty, but never misses a date
They tell me she's 'ugly', with nowhere to go
& maybe that's why, I'm in love with her so!

Mercutio

And still you spoke
of nothing

And your thoughts so often
passed us by –

For a dream of love you borrowed
Cupid's wings

and Queen Mab's chariot
to draw your words

in the likeness of a sigh …

How could your gallant spirit die?
when a single prayer from your
idle brain

would make us all believe

My friend, you left with
no goodbye –

And how I mourn your mischievous rhyme!

For what is life without our dreams?

and we all know, that dreamers never lie ...

Steven J. Scott

The Waiting

You tap your fingers
on the bar
and hope that she will
show her face

She keeps you waiting
for her smile
keeps you rooted
in your place

You shuffle feet
and try to look at ease
surely
she will be here soon?

You order another
awkwardly
trying not to glance
around the room

And as time ticks by
you start to think
that maybe you've been
here before

But with gloom descending
in your glass
you hear her laughter
at the door.

Flower Girl

The flower girl smiles at me
outside the station, in the rain
it's early evening, the sky is dark

people rushing for the trains

I think of you, and forget the crowd
suddenly I feel okay
the flower girl smiles at me

perhaps I'll take a small bouquet?

Scrooge

The spirits haunt me all my life
they came to visit in the night

Alone I sat with a bowl of gruel
wrapped in my cloak of solitude

Oh! What errors I have made!
locked away from mankind –

And all the time a ponderous chain
pulled my sins along behind …

Bill Sikes

Sometimes the frenzy overtakes me
the inner despair

the indignity

To thieve all my days
for the right to live

While the rich sit in their drawing rooms
and contemplate their finery ...

In the Reptile House

I'm always nervous
standing here

Even though I know
you can't escape

It's much too warm and I start
to sweat

I've always had this fear
of snakes …

My skin starts crawling as I test
the lock

Coiled in the corner of a brittle
cage

Your eyes seem to fix
on me –

Knowing, soon
the glass will break …

Diesel

Diesel fills up at our cold narrow streets
While I shiver beneath the traffic-light glare
The city recoils under dirty burnt tyres
Squealing out for a purpose, in the night sky

The rainy, clammy, smoggy air
The fumy embrace of the kettle-drum fires
The putrid stench of slow dripping drains
Pours out of our mouths and back in again …

Diesel is dragging on fragile nerve ends
Pushing poisonous smoke through the lungs of our breath
Rows of commuters in shuffling queues –
Closed circuit TV, tracking edited news

The sky thickly layered in dust diesel clouds
Smothers the city in its strong grimy hand
Holding it hostage to an ill-lit desire
An oily exchange on the lamps of our palms

As I walk through the streets there are shapes on the ground
So many homeless in cardboard-box land
Diesel is choking the pulse of our lives
And compassion is drowning, deep in the mire ...

Of diesel.

Dry-Dock

The basement bar was dull & dark
a bleary girl danced
the soft beat of desire
her silhouette clung to the walls
slowly seducing our spirits
on ice

The place reeked of quiet
corruption
I picked up my hat
& stepped out alone
the rain tapped a melody
upon the low rooftops & cobblestones

A cold wind whispered off the docks
something was missing –
something was wrong
in the hotel mirror I stared at a stranger
& wondered where a lifetime
had gone.

Raptors

Remorseless eyes search
the jungle night

waiting for the wind to change

Bird-like claws tap patiently –
from a killer's grasp there's no escape

And now – attack!
so fast, so sure

A swift embrace and flesh
is torn

Then all grows quiet as they feed
in a blood-red

prehistoric dawn.

Debris

It was scattered
all over
the buildings destroyed
the inhabitants gone

Shards of a history
denied and wiped out
shattered glass
and broken bone

And all that remained
in the fading light
was the howling of ghosts
whose tears could not fall

And the mutterings
of a crazed machine
still lazily swinging its
wrecking-ball.

Selected Poems & The Lost Drabbles

Tapestries

A mist surrounds the castle walls
Harsh trumpets sound the call to war

Brave knights ride out beyond the gates
To live or die upon their swords

A raven in the tower croaks
A bitter tale of endless strife

Forbidden love and destiny
Honour, treachery, desire …

In quiet chambers ladies sew
Embroidering the tapestries

Their nimble fingers pull the threads
Who knows what pattern

Fate will weave?

Hamlet

Ghostly conscience
haunts his steps

Vengeance stalks
a bitter stage

Where flights of angels
bow their heads

Sick at heart …
and betrayed

Barbarians

Kings and chieftains
ruled the tribal lands

With pagan swords
and iron hands

Craftsmen worked in wood and stone
shaping spears and shields

and golden bows

Worshipping their grim-faced gods
the talisman and mystic runes

Unsettled nomad wanderers
shrouded in time's distant hues

Tribes spread out in glowing clans
and would not bow
to any rule

The Goths sacked a dying Rome
her Empire about to fall ...

And looking back on all we've learned
have our battles been in vain?

Will our passion see us through
or lead us to a new Dark Age?

The Ninth Legion

Five thousand men unaccounted for
eagle standard trails in a northern breeze

No monuments for the lost legion
no graves, no bones, no antiquity

But sometimes when
the moon is high

I wonder if they've really
gone

Or maybe they still stand their watch
upon the hills of Avalon?

Steven J. Scott

Grendel

Unseen
I wait for night to fall
and watch the heroes at their mead
in many battles have they fought
seeking fame and honour
for their deeds

But now their laughter
is subdued
and terror clutches at their minds
in fitful sleep I slay them all
a blood-feud since the dawn
of time

Brave warriors are
dwindling
despair now stalks their silent halls
twitching hands on useless swords –
unseen, I wait for night
to fall.

Museum

Each gallery holds a precious
secret
a turn in evolution's wheel
eyeless skulls stare back at us
their ghosts in cabinets
neatly sealed

Trapped inside this
labyrinth
time betrays our passing years
and we're blindly groping for the exit
with our bag of plastic
souvenirs.

Steven J. Scott

Spider

Spider crawls across my floor
he does not bother me
but he knows I've seen him and stops dead

Later he climbs and so nearly reaches the top
and falls – I try to help
but I cannot hold him without breaking something

I know he is frightened

All of life is in his silence
but I would not harm the spider
for I only harm myself

Like me, he is searching
looking for a place to hide in the shadows

and all I can do is watch him struggle
for our freedom.

Snow

Sitting patiently behind the glass
of shop window as snow falls
outside

smiling statue of Buddha.

The Haunting of Emily

She hurries down a narrow street
speeding up
her haunted steps

A cry is muffled in the smog
a heartbeat missed –
a soul at rest

On the Thames the boats are tied
the river silent

moonlight still

Big Ben strikes a midnight chime
another hour ... and all
is well

Upon her shoulder, the lightest touch
but turning
she sees nothing there

Only the ghost of a hansom cab
waiting
for the Devil's fare.

Love Song in the Night (New York, 1942)

It's 2am
and the crowd is hushed
as she glides onto the stage

Smoke rings settle, lights are dimmed –
she looks unreal in pearls
and lace

The mood is slow
while the bass begins to
purr around the room

And a blues piano
softly hints
at a soulful mellow tune

She starts to sing
and soon my mind is far away
with her gentle hymn of longing

Living every pain
every love that's gone
astray

A waiter whispers in my ear –
but her voice has opened
up my heart

And the only sound that I can hear
is her sweet love song
in the night.

Odyssey

We have been to a foreign place
in a foreign time
and now our wanderings are done
we have returned to our homeland -
so many battles lost
and won

And how could we fight destiny?
how were we to read the signs?
when all that we believed
was wrong
all we loved, beyond our reach –
all we hoped for
gone ...

So yes, we have returned
but we are not the same
as when we left these shores –
our faith is marred by suffering
and we cling to fading memories
that drift away like a lover's kiss ...

through the ivory gates of dream.

The Lost Drabbles

Sammy Squirrel Takes a Risk

Sammy Squirrel took a final look around the drey he was about to leave.

It had been a good drey, the first he had built, and now he was taking his family into the Great Forest.

Sammy knew this was a risk. It would be a long, hazardous journey, and he couldn't be certain if the forest creatures would welcome them or not.

Still, there were no guarantees of safety wherever they went, and Sammy was no stranger to adventures – he had no regrets.

"Goodbye, old place," he whispered.

And Sammy smiled, quietly closed the door, and didn't look back.

Mr. Po's Old Comrade

Mr. Po climbed the last step of the ladder into the dusty attic.

The Seafarer's Inn was quiet this evening, and his friend, Mr. Yu, was running the bar, while he made final preparations for the voyage ahead.

Mr. Po smiled when he thought back to his days as a young adventurer and buccaneer ... how many years ago?

Finally, at the bottom of an ancient sea chest, he found it.

"Ah, my beauty!" he exclaimed, and with a tear in his eye he held his old cutlass up, and it glimmered as it caught the light from his flickering candle.

The Seventh Gate

The handsome young prince rode into the castle, seeking the beautiful princess for his bride. The old king welcomed the prince, and gave him a task:

"Here are seven keys to the kingdom. In the forest, you will encounter seven gates. Unlock the first six and enter – but on no account open the seventh gate!"

But the prince did not return, and in her tower, the princess heard his awful scream, for, despite her beauty, she was an evil enchantress, who did not wish to marry, and had placed a dreadful curse upon the prince – to enter the seventh gate!

The Dream Tea of the Emperor Hu

And in the leaves he saw himself, playing in the gardens as a child.

He was running to and fro, in a game of 'hide and seek', searching for his friends among the shadows.

Suddenly his parents were there, on the balcony, calling him inside, as the sun set in the peaceful valley.

But the kingdom grew tired.

War was being forged.

Soon the nightingales would sing no more.

And when the Emperor woke from his day-dream he was weeping, for all he dreamed of had long since perished, and he was powerless to stop the passing of the years.

Spider & Fly

I'm trying to lure you in.

I weave the web out silkily from the edges of my nerves.

And I sit, so quietly.

It's the perfect trap.

In the morning dew you wouldn't even know I was waiting, about to ensnare you in a gentle vice of gossamer thread.

Quietly now ... I can sense your fear – but it won't take long, no need to struggle – just a slight incision and you'll be numb.

You cannot fight back, you cannot shake loose. You only waste your energy.

A little closer ... you're almost there.

Just rest, in the arms of my pincers.

The City of Tears

We came down from the mountains and beheld the City of Tears.

We felt her loneliness and heard her silence, and knew not what to do. We tried to comfort her, but it was no use.

The city knew only sorrow.

Her once bustling streets were empty.

Her once thriving markets closed.

Her once proud flags were lowered, and sad wreaths lay upon her stones.

So we led her weeping soul away, as imprisoned eyes watched through hollow doors, and our vision blurred through the ghostly rain.

For her past had been diminished, and her golden future was no more.

The Duchess's Diamonds

The gentleman thief turned, with a disarming smile, and met the famous detective's gaze.

"A pleasant surprise!"

"I do hope so. Of course, I know you did it."

"I'm sorry?"

"The theft of the Duchess's diamonds. At the time of the burglary you were batting at Lords, nevertheless, I know you are the culprit."

"But you could never ..."

"I do not *wish* to prove it. You are exonerated in this affair."

"How so?"

"You scored a century, I believe?"

"Ah, yes."

"Well, we defeated the abominable Australians, did we not?"

And they both grinned, and shook hands (gloved, of course).

Sour

The fox was very hungry.

He'd been searching all day for something to eat, but had found only scraps.

He was on his way home, when he spotted a row of grapes on a vine, but when he leapt up to reach them, he found they were just beyond his grasp.

But the fox was clever, and soon found an old discarded box, which he pushed under the vine, and clambered up.

This time he could easily reach the grapes, but when he tasted them, he quickly spat them out.

"Ugh, disgusting!" he exclaimed – for the grapes were horribly sour.

Dreadful Penny

I tumbled down the bloody drain, and lay for years rotting in the dark, until some putrid water carried me, through filthy sewers, along rusting pipes, and back onto the London streets.

A drunken sailor found me then, and in a grimy alley I changed hands. And so I rested in a woman's purse, and felt quite safe there for a while, mixed with others of my kind.

But then one night she walked alone, and Jack the Shadow followed her.

A shallow smile – a sharpened blade – and amidst the horror and the screams ... I tumbled down the bloody drain!

The Ogre's House

Floorboards creak, and the air is stale.

It's hard to breathe in here, and my heart beats faster, as I feel his presence all around.

Huge cobwebs hang from massive wooden beams above, and the walls feel damp and cold, as if they were closing in on me.

I gaze out of a broken window, and can just make out a narrow pathway, leading to the sea. Life has fallen into dust here ... and yet, I dare not make a sound.

I feel a sudden chill, and hear a heavy footstep in the dark.

> Outside, the wolves begin to howl.

The Captain's Table

The first officer was speaking:

"It was a bitter night, my first on watch. All was quiet, and the sea was so still. It was then that I saw it – the spectre – the Jonah! I looked on in terror, as it tore at the mainsail, and tugged at the shrouds, wailing and weeping."

He drank deeply, and stared at the pale faces around him.

"Sometimes I can hear its voice in my head, calling to me …"

And on they talked, of spirits and ghouls, as their battered ship lay on the ocean floor, the cold black waters swirling around her.

Arena

In the Colosseum, the runaway slave is pushed forward by the guards.

He is thin and ragged, and his eyes can barely focus on the baying crowd.

From out of nowhere, a lion's roar brings a gasp from the arena. And then silence. He falls on his knees, his body convulsing with fear.

He tries to pray, "Oh Lord, receive my spirit." He feels the words, but cannot speak.

There is a slow dragging of chains, and a cage is opened.

He lifts his head, to look upon death … and it nudges him gently, and holds out its hungry paw.

The Witch

Wild and alone, she wanders these hills.

The glimpse of a veil, you cannot be sure …

A cool sweat on your brow, a gasp in your throat, your heartbeat so loud.

In the village, nobody speaks of the past, but you feel a storm brewing – the turn of the tide, the bark of a fox, the swoop of an owl.

She visits your dreams, in the depth of the night, desire and horror tormenting your mind.

And then she is gone, inscrutable as mist on a lake. You've seen her before – but in the morning you cannot remember her face.

Loose Ends

So, I went back to clear a few things up.

Closure.

That's what they call it now. But that's bullshit. It wasn't 'closure' – it was revenge.

I took the wrong turn on the wrong road. Maybe it was a personal duel, but it didn't matter.

I had to go back.

I drove that bike all night, the wind singing through my leather jacket like a long-lost rock tune, and the water in my eyes made me see clearer.

Destiny – it's all about that in the end. We can't control it, it just happens.

I had to go back.

Closure, yeah.

The Trail

"Don't go into town, Billy."

"Why boss?"

"It's a bad town, bad men, bad liquor – bad women."

"Well, boss, you know, it's been a long time …"

"There's another town three days from here."

"Three more days of roping and chasing cattle – and this heat! Boss, I'm trail sick!"

"Three more days, Billy."

They made camp near the stream. The men slept under the stars. By dawn, the rains had come.

"Boss! Billy – he's gone!"

"Damned fool! I told him."

"The town – we should go in after him."

"No, we keep moving."

"But boss …"

"He made his choice. Now, saddle up!"

Demon Drive

He drove on through the night.

Where was he going? He couldn't remember. He only knew he had to keep driving.

The road was narrow and winding. The rain lashed down in torrents. Trees seemed to reach out, clawing, and a banshee wind screeched and howled.

Darkness smothered everything.

Despite all this, he was driving faster, and as he drove, his mind began to clear.

Oh yes, he remembered now – the crimson robes, the sacrifice, her terrified eyes – and he remembered who he was, and what was in the boot …

He laughed out loud, and drove on towards the gates.

The Hunt

And the tiger hunts.

His camouflage matches the tall grass.

The gazelle snorts and sniffs the air. She can sense that something is wrong, something moving just outside the line of her vision.

She stands perfectly still.

The tiger edges closer, almost in range – just a few more paces ...

She twitches nervously, her hoof scratches the dry ground.

The tiger stops – watches her eyes. Silence shrieks from the tree-tops.

And then he leaps!

She panics – twists – stumbles in the dust ...

A flock of squawking birds rise into the air, chaotic in their terror.

A drifting cloud veils the blood-red moon.

The Archive

No one ever visited the isolated monastery, or consulted its ancient archive, and the monks eyed the impatient soldiers nervously.

Their young leader had been persistent.

Father Cuthbert knelt in his cell and prayed. Somehow he felt the world was about to change forever.

Finally, his guest was ready to leave, and Father Cuthbert met him in the courtyard.

"Did you find what you needed?"

"Oh yes. I know what to do now."

As the soldiers rode off, one of the novices asked: "Who was he, Father?"

But Father Cuthbert slowly closed the register over the name.

Alexander of Macedon.

Between Stations

The train rumbles on through the night.

She leans back in her seat, and watches her distorted reflection in the window, as another station flashes by in the darkness.

A long journey north – hour after hour.

She's tried to keep her mind occupied, but too much reading, and the music in her headphones, has given her a headache.

Her destination is cloudy, and somehow remote. The stone walls of her college, the draughty lecture halls, her hastily scribbled notes …

She closes her eyes, tired, but unable to sleep.

She's caught between dreaming and waking, between shadows and light.

Between stations.

Panic at Dodge City!

"This is bad, sheriff."

The deputy was pale and jittery.

In the raucous saloon the gambling tables were crowded, young women were loitering, another fight had broken out, and a honky-tonk piano tinkled – a fairly average night in Dodge.

The sheriff rubbed his stubby chin, "I can't believe it, after all this time – are you sure?"

"Oh yes, word is, he's been sent to clean up the town, he could be here at any ..."

Suddenly everything went quiet, and they knew it was over, as fifty robot heads turned to the doorway and saw a tall silhouette – a *human* silhouette.

Smith & Jones

Back at the station, Sergeant Smith was being grilled by Inspector Jones.

"Was he beat up bad?"

"I hardly recognized him, sir. He looked like a piece of glitch art."

"Very droll, sergeant. Did he say anything?"

"Hard to talk when you haven't got any teeth, and your jaw's in a sling, sir."

"What about the other case – any clues?"

"Oh, yes sir, it was the poisoned loaf that killed him."

"A poisoned loaf! Tragic."

"Another one bites the crust, sir."

"Sergeant – you have missed your true vocation!"

"Sir?"

"Why, you're a comedian, Sergeant Smith."

"And you're a joke, sir."

Smith & Jones (Part 2)

"That's enough of your insolence, Sergeant Smith."

"Yessir. There was one more case, sir."

"Well?"

"The case of the Mangled Cat, sir."

"Mangled cat! What happened?"

"Well, first it was drenched in the storm, then it was nearly frozen in the snow, and finally it was caught in a blaze, and set on fire."

"But this is terrible!"

"We sent for the fire brigade, and they had to put their hoses on it."

"Oh, the poor creature! Did it survive?"

"Creature? Oh, well, the Mangled Cat is a pub, sir."

"Get out of here, Smith – you're on traffic duty – forever!"

Smugglers

A lantern clicked on in the dark.

And slowly they pulled the boats up the beach, and hauled the barrels towards the sinister caves.

Nervously, they looked about, and tried not to think of the soldiers and guns, the men rotting on gibbets all along the coast.

Shadows and rumours – you trusted no one. For the price of a pardon, your friends turned to foes.

Only by moonlight their shapes could be seen, like lingering ghosts of forgotten pirates, returning to haunt this deserted bay.

And out at sea, watching for a signal from shore, a tall ship waited restlessly.

Decorating

Lou is cleaning the glasses as Harvey appears at the bar.

Lou pulls Harvey his usual pint, and, seeing that Harvey is in a bad mood, attempts to cheer him up:

"How's the decorating going, Harv?"

"Oh, not so bad."

"Have you finished yet?"

"Yeah, I only got the living room, kitchen, bathroom, and bedroom to do."

"But that's all there is!"

"Yeah, I said it was going well."

Lou sighs, and pulls another beer. Harvey is the best detective on the force, but nobody has ever told him so.

A rumble of thunder, and the rain starts to fall.

Geometry

Triangle: Well, it looks all right at first, but then you start to wonder, for every way you turn, its sharp edges are pointing at you.

Square: This is a bit claustrophobic, there's no room to manoeuvre. I don't really like it. I'm feeling nervous, and I need to get out, but I'm trapped here, boxed-in.

Circle: It seems quite easy, nothing to fear, but after a while you realise you're not going anywhere, and slowly, you start to panic. It's like a Ferris wheel that you can't get off – it just keeps turning you around, and around … and around …

Crooked

"You're tired, and you're not thinking straight."

"I know, but there's no law against thinking crooked, is there?"

"So, what are we going to do?"

"Think."

"We don't have much time."

"Be quiet!"

"I'm only trying to help, and you get all …"

"How can I think when you keep on talking?"

"Okay – I'll say nothing then!"

"Good!"

"How are we going to get out of this?"

"By thinking about it."

"How did we get caught in the first place?"

"We were unlucky."

"Will we be all right?"

"I don't know."

"What can I do to help?"

"Shut up!"

"Okay … but …"

Code of Honour

The knights faced each other, as a fog drifted in from the lake.

They dismounted, and drew their swords. A weak sun glinted on their armour.

No words were spoken, they both knew this was a fight to the death. They cried out, and their heavy swords clashed, swiping and lunging.

As the mist rose, a castle could be seen across the lake, and a rainbow appeared in the sky. The fight continued, but one of the knights stumbled, and his sword fell to the ground.

His opponent backed away.

"Pick it up."

A moment later, their swords clashed again.

Pebbles

After centuries of war, the inter-galactic peace treaty was signed.

The celebrations would last forever.

Prince Max turned joyfully to his nephew: "This is the greatest day in history!"

There were tears in his eyes when the skies lit up in a beautiful silver glow, as each space fleet's plasma display acknowledged a new era of peace …

The child was searching for crabs in the rock pools, but could find only pebbles. In her plastic bucket, a tiny silver pebble sparkled brightly, and caught her eye.

She sighed in frustration, and with her little spade, ground the pebbles into dust.

Tresses

Her maid is so gentle, as the ebony comb glides through her tresses, and she closes her eyes while her hair is loosened, falling and flowing.

She is falling into a dream …

Curtains of silk surround the soft bed, and moonlight shines through the open window, leaving its glow on the scented pillows and sheets.

The royal palace is sleeping, there is peace in the land, and the Empress sighs as the maid bows her head and kisses her once on her outstretched hand.

"Don't leave."

"Your majesty?"

"Stay with me."

And the maid begins again, and stays until dawn.

Step

For centuries we had found nothing.

From the earliest missions, to the deep space exploration vessels that had charted over a thousand new worlds – the emptiness remained.

We were alone in the universe.

We discovered only ourselves, our own weaknesses, our own limitations, our own pettiness and stupidities.

We discovered how small we were. An insignificant race, desperately searching for a purpose, a meaning to things.

But nobody heard or saw us, until, on a far distant moon, an ancient scanner picked up the strange sound of an alien voice:

"One small step …"

We are on our way to investigate.

www.ingramcontent.com/pod-product-compliance
Lightning Source LLC
Chambersburg PA
CBHW050303120526
44590CB00016B/2465